R

DISCARD

THE
FOLLETT
BEGINNING TO READ
SERIES

A FOLLETT BEGINNING · TO · READ BOOK

FOLLETT BEGINNING·TO·READ

Library of Congress Catalog Card Number: 59—13400

Alta McIntire Formerly Director of Primary Education
and Curriculum, Public Schools, Berwyn, Illinois.
Author of many books for children,
and educational consultant.

Illustrated by **Janet LaSalle**

PICTURE
DICTIONARY

Follett Publishing Company · Chicago

©Follett Publishing Company 1959
Manufactured in the United States of America
345678910

4

 A a

airplane

animals

ant

apple

arm

B b

baby

ball

barn

bear

bed

bicycle

birds

birthday cake

black

a b c d e f g h i j k l m n o p q r s t u v w x y z

blue

boat

book

boy

bread

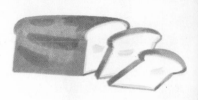

breakfast

brown

bus

butterfly

candy

buttons

cat

C c

chair

camel

chicken

a b c d e f g h i j k l m n o p q r s t u v w x y z

children

city

Christmas tree

clock

coat

church

cooky

country

dime

dinner

cow

D d

doctor

dentist

dog

doll

drum

dollar

duck

door

E e

dress

ear

Easter eggs

eye

eight

F f

face

elephant

fall

engine

family

father

feet

fire

fish

five

5

flag

flowers

four

4 ::

girl

fruit

grass

G g

giraffe

gray

green

H h

hat

hair

head

Halloween party

hippopotamus

hand

14

horse

Indian

house

J j

jacket

 I i

ice cream

jelly

a b c d e f g h i j k l m n o p q r s t u v w x y z

K k

kangaroo

kitchen

key

kite

king

kitten

L l

leaves

lion

legs

lunch

M m

letter

mailbox

a b c d e f g h i j k **l** m n o p q r s t u v w x y z

man

monkey

meat

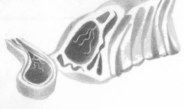

moon

milk

mother

money

mouth

N n

nest

nickel

nine

nose

numbers

1 2 3 5 6 8 0
  4   7 9

nurse

nuts

a b c d e f g h i j k l m n o p q r s t u v w x y z

O o

one

orange

owl

P p

penny

people

pig

police car

queen

pumpkin

R r

rabbit

Q q

quarter

rain

red

robin

school

S s

seven

7

Santa Claus

sheep

shoe

spider

six

spring

snake

squirrel

snow

star

a b c d e f g h i j k l m n o p q r s t u v w x y z

street

swing

T t

summer

table

sun

teacher

teeth

ten

Thanksgiving
turkey

three

toys

train

truck

turtle

two

U u

umbrella

uniform

V v

valentine

vegetables

W w

wagon

watch

wheel

whistle

water

window

winter

whale

witch

woman

X x

xylophone

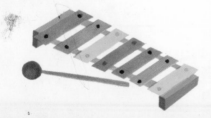

Y y

yard

yarn

yellow

zipper

zebra

zoo

zero

Here are sentences for you to read.
The words in blue are in the dictionary.

A cow is a farm animal.
A giraffe is a zoo animal.
An elephant is a big animal.
A cat is a little animal.
Mother is in the kitchen.
Father is in the yard.

The swing is in the yard.
The swing can go up and down.
The children play in the yard with the dog.
See the little house for the dog.
See the big house for the people.
The little house is green.

The big house is yellow.
An orange is fruit.
Look at the red apple.
Fruit is good for my lunch.
Milk is good for you and me at breakfast.

We want vegetables and meat for dinner.
We see the milk in the truck.
We look at the man in the truck.
The children go to the store with money.
Mother said the money is for bread and milk.
A penny and a nickel are money.

A dime and a quarter are money.
A dollar is money.
I have a little cat.
My little cat can come in the house.
You have a big brown dog.
The big dog can not come in the house.

Mother can make a dress and coat for me.
Mother said she can make a jacket for you.
Mother can make a jacket with a zipper.
A zipper can go up and down.
Mother and Father work for the family.

Using the Beginning-to-Read PICTURE DICTIONARY

The pictures in this beginners' dictionary illustrate basic words in the primary vocabulary. The vocabulary deals with: *Animals, Clothing, Colors, Community Helpers, Family Life, Holidays, House and Home, Kinds of Food, Meals, Money, Numbers, Parts of the Body, People, Plants, Recreation, Seasons, Vehicles, Weather.*

The type used for the vocabulary is the same manuscript writing which most children learn before they learn cursive writing. It will be familiar to the first grade child, and may serve as a guide in his own writing.

The words were chosen because of their importance in daily living as well as their usefulness in written and spoken language and their familiarity to the child.

Some of the most necessary words in the primary vocabulary can not be illustrated. The easiest way for children to learn these words is in context. For this reason, many of them are presented in sentences, each of which includes one or more words from the picture dictionary. This gives added value to the sentences, since they require recognition of the dictionary words in context. These words are printed in color to tell children that they can be found in the dictionary. The following words are in the sentences but not in the picture dictionary:

a	come	here	me	the
an	down	I	my	to
and	farm	in	not	up
are	for	is	play	want
at	go	little	said	we
big	good	look	see	with
can	have	make	she	work
			store	you